# Wood

Written by Jo Windsor

## CONTENTS

# What Are Wood Storks?

Wood storks are large birds that live by water.
Wood storks grow to about one metre tall.
They use their long, skinny legs to wade
through the water, looking for food.

# flyers and fishers

Wood storks are good at flying and fishing.
They can fly high into the air and then glide
a long way with their head and legs out.
Wood storks can dive, roll and turn in the sky.

These pictures show a wood stork coming in to land.

# Fishing by Feeling

Wood storks have long beaks that are very good for finding fish in the water where they live. They move their open beaks through the muddy water to feel for small fish. At the same time, they use their feet to scare fish up from the bottom. When a bird feels a fish, it snaps its beak shut on it.

Wood storks also eat frogs, snakes and crayfish.

frogs

fish

Wood stork food

snakes

crayfish

# Nesting Wood Storks

Wood storks like to stay together. They nest in groups. They are careful about where they build their nests. They have enemies, like racoons. They can build their nests on islands or in tall trees hanging over the water.

Sometimes many wood storks nest in one tree. They often fight for a place in the tree. They clap their bills and snap their wings.

The alligator helps the wood stork. It catches racoons, which are the wood stork's enemies.

# Nest Building

Wood storks build their nests in the dry season. Some birds build new nests and some find old, empty nests and fix these up. Wood storks work together to build their nests. The male bird finds all the things it needs for the nest. The female makes the nest.

## Nest Materials

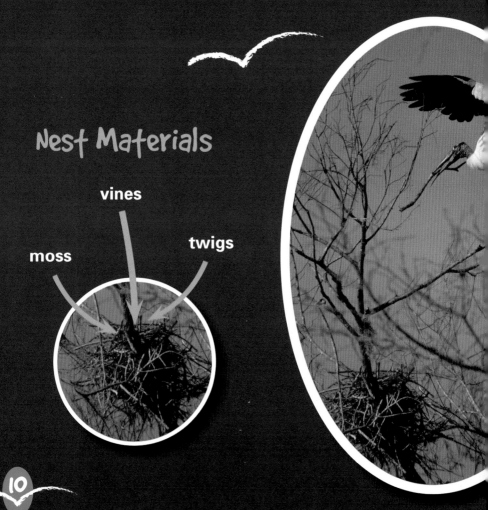

vines

moss

twigs

# Eggs and Chicks

Wood storks look after their chicks very well. The female lays three to five eggs in the nest. Both wood stork parents share the job of keeping the eggs warm. When the eggs hatch, the parents work hard to find food for their chicks. They may fly a long way each day, looking for food.

The birds feed their chicks by eating fish and spitting it out into the nest. When they are about two months old, the chicks will be ready to leave the nest.

# Watching Out for Wood Storks

There are not as many wood storks as there used to be. Scientists are watching the wood storks and finding out where they go.

The scientists catch the birds and put transmitters on them. The transmitters get information about where the birds fly.

The scientists look at the information and try to learn more about these birds. Then they can help other wood storks.

## Glossary

transmitters – special tools used for getting information

transmitter

**Size** – wood storks are one metre tall. They have long, skinny legs to wade in water.

**Flying** – wood storks glide, dive, roll and turn in the sky.

**Eggs and chicks** – the female lays three to five eggs in the nest. Both parents look after the eggs and chicks.

**Wood Storks**

**Nesting** – wood storks nest in trees or on islands.

# Index

**Fishing** – wood storks scare fish up with their feet and catch them in their beaks.

# Reports

**Wood Storks** is a **Report**.

**A report has a topic:**

> # Wood Storks

**A report has headings:**

## What Are Wood Storks?

## Flyers and Fishers

## Nesting Wood Storks

## Watching Out for Wood Storks

18

# Some information is put under headings.

## flyers and fishers

**Wood storks are good at flying and fishing.**

**Wood storks have long beaks that are very good for finding fish.**

## Information can be shown in other ways. This report has . . .

Labels

Photographs

Captions

Photographic Web

Diagrams

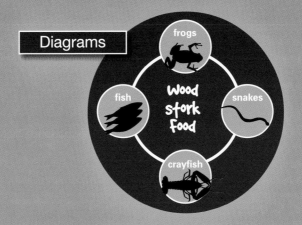

frogs

Wood stork food

fish

snakes

crayfish

# Guide Notes

**Title: Wood Storks**

**Stage:** Fluency

**Text Form:** Informational Report

**Approach:** Guided Reading

**Processes:** Thinking Critically, Exploring Language, Processing Information

**Written and Visual Focus:** Captions, Labels, Index, Contents Page, Glossary, Illustrative Diagrams, Photographic Web

## THINKING CRITICALLY
(sample questions)

### Before Reading – Establishing Prior Knowledge
· What do you know about wood storks?

### Visualising the Text Content
· What might you expect to see in this book?
· What form of writing do you think will be used by the author?

Look at the contents page and index. Encourage the students to think about the information and make predictions about the text content.

### After Reading – Interpreting the Text
· Why do you think having long, skinny legs helps the wood stork?
· Why do you think wood storks like to stay together in groups?
· Why do you think there are not as many wood storks as there used to be?
· What do you know about the wood stork that you didn't know before?
· What things in the book helped you understand the information?
· What questions do you have after reading the text?

## EXPLORING LANGUAGE

### Terminology
Photograph credits, index, contents page, imprint information, ISBN number

### Vocabulary
**Clarify:** wade, enemies, season, parents, scientists, transmitters, information
**Nouns:** wood stork, beaks, fish, nests
**Verbs:** wade, fly, snaps, build
**Singular/plural:** wood stork/wood storks, foot/feet, enemy/enemies
Focus the students' attention on **adjectives, homonyms, antonyms** and **synonyms** if appropria